CLEVER COOKIE CUTTER

3 COOKIE CUTTERS
30 CREATIVE DESIGNS

JEN RICH

An Hachette UK Company
www.hachette.co.uk

First published in Great Britain in 2022
by Pyramid, an imprint of
Octopus Publishing Group Ltd
Carmelite House
50 Victoria Embankment
London, EC4Y 0DZ
www.octopusbooks.co.uk

Distributed in the US by
Hachette Book Group
1290 Avenue of the Americas
4th and 5th Floors
New York, NY 10104

Distributed in Canada by
Canadian Manda Group
664 Annette St.
Toronto, Ontario, Canada M6S 2C8

ISBN: 978-0-7537-3485-8

A CIP catalogue record for this book is
available from the British Library

Printed and bound in China

10 9 8 7 6 5 4 3 2 1

Publisher: Lucy Pessell
Designer: Hannah Coughlin
Editor: Sarah Kennedy
Editorial Assistant: Emily Martin
Photographer and stylist: Jen Rich
Production Controller: Katherine Hockley

UK / US GLOSSARY

baking tray – baking sheet
icing sugar – confectioners' sugar
plain flour – all-purpose flour

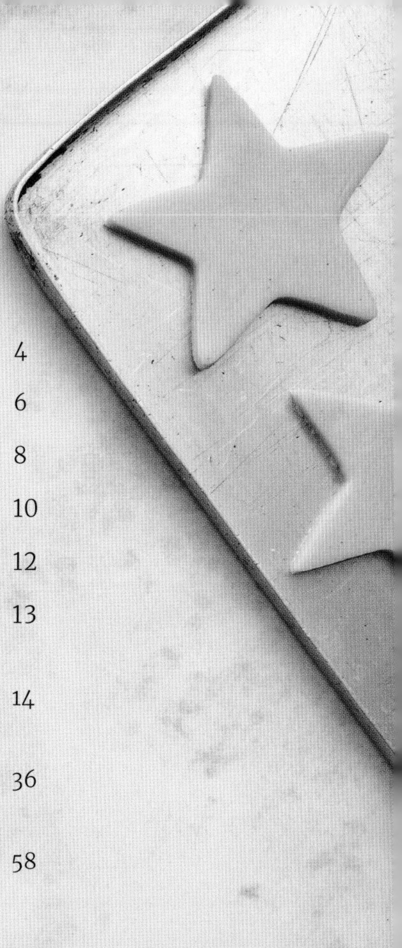

CONTENTS

INTRODUCTION   4

    COOKIE BASE RECIPE   6

    TYPES OF ICING   8

    PIPING YOUR ICING   10

    EQUIPMENT   12

    TIPS AND TRICKS   13

HEART CUTTER   14

GINGERBREAD MAN CUTTER   36

STAR CUTTER   58

INTRODUCTION

Whether you're new to cookie decorating or not, *Clever Cookie Cutter* has everything you need to know in order to get started. And the best thing about the cookie designs in this book is that all it takes is just three simple, everyday cookie cutters you probably already have lying around in your kitchen cupboards: a heart, a gingerbread man and a star. Creating gorgeous and impressive-looking cookies has never been easier.

This book is split into three sections, each of which corresponds to the cookie-cutter shape you are using. For each design, start with your freshly baked (and cooled) cookie, and make sure you have all the icing and equipment you need ready to go. Before you begin, make sure you read through the next few pages. They include basic cookie and icing recipes, useful bits of equipment, and lots of handy tips and tricks.

If you're new to cookie decorating, start with the simpler designs – such as the alien on page 38, or the tie-dye design on page 67 – and go from there. And when you move on to the more complicated cookies, don't worry if your designs don't look great at first. The more you practise, the better you will get. And, hey, you get to eat all the practice cookies you make, so it's always a win-win situation.

If you're decorating cookies as a gift, a lot of the designs in this book pair up nicely to make beautiful, themed gift boxes. And don't forget to experiment as much as you like with different colours and variations of the designs. You don't have to stick to exactly how they appear in the book. Let your imagination run wild, and – most importantly – have fun!

COOKIE BASE RECIPE

This dough recipe generally makes enough for about six cookies, depending on the cookie-cutter size. The quantity can easily be doubled to make a larger batch.

WHAT YOU'LL NEED

150 g (5½ oz) plain flour, plus extra for dusting

100 g (3½ oz) lightly salted firm butter, diced

50 g (1¾ oz) icing sugar

1 egg yolk

1 teaspoon vanilla extract or vanilla bean paste

1. Put the flour and butter in a food processor and blend until the mixture resembles fine breadcrumbs. Briefly blend in the icing sugar.

2. Add the egg yolk and vanilla and blend again until the mixture comes together to make a smooth dough.

3. Alternatively, to make the dough by hand, place the flour and butter in a bowl and mix with your fingertips until the mixture resembles fine breadcrumbs, then add the remaining ingredients and knead into a smooth dough.

4. Turn the dough out onto a lightly floured surface and knead gently to incorporate any stray crumbs. Wrap in clingfilm and chill for at least 1 hour before rolling.

5. Roll out the cookie dough on a lightly floured surface to about 5 mm (¼ in) thick. If the dough is too firm to roll, leave it to stand at room temperature for 20–30 minutes. The firmer the dough when you roll it, the less likely it will lose its shape during baking.

6. Cut out shapes using your chosen cutter. Dusting the cookie cutter with flour will help make a clean, non-sticky cut. The remaining dough can then be gathered up, lightly kneaded and re-rolled to make extra shapes.

7. Place the shapes on a lightly greased baking tray, spacing them slightly apart to allow for spreading. Bake in a preheated oven at 190°C (375°F), Gas Mark 5 for 12–15 minutes.

Plain cookies will be done when they start turning golden around the edges. Chocolate cookies (see below) will look baked, but will not darken much.

8. Remove the cookies from the oven and leave on the baking tray for 2 minutes before transferring to a wire rack. The high sugar content of the cookies means they will be slightly soft when they come out of the oven and will crisp up as they cool.

FLAVOUR VARIATIONS

To create a different visual effect, you can adjust the cookie flavours for different coloured bases.

GINGER COOKIES
Replace the icing sugar with light brown sugar and add 1 teaspoon of ground ginger instead of the vanilla.

CHOCOLATE COOKIES
Replace 25 g (1 oz) of the flour with 25 g (1 oz) of cocoa powder.

LEMON COOKIES
Add the finely grated zest of 1 lemon and replace the vanilla with 1 teaspoon of lemon juice.

TYPES OF ICING

The icing used to decorate the cookies throughout this book is royal icing, and there are three different consistencies used for different steps and techniques, and to achieve different effects. The three types you need to be familiar with are detailed below.

You can use either shop bought royal icing sugar and make it up according to the packet instructions, or give making your own a try. Start with the basic royal icing opposite, and then either add a little more icing sugar to make the icing stiffer, or add a few drops of water to make it thinner. Be careful to add only very small amounts of water at a time.

If the recipe requires small amounts of piped icing, tubes of icing make a good substitute and come in various colours.

FLOOD ICING

This is used to fill in large shapes on your cookies. Flooding gives a smooth and professional-looking finish to which you can add further decorations.You'll know you have the perfect consistency when it takes about 10 seconds to settle into a flat layer. Pipe the icing into the area you wish to flood, and spread it into the corners with a cocktail stick if necessary.

PIPING ICING

This is used to pipe slightly more detailed, smaller shapes. It should take about 15 seconds to settle into a flat layer.

DETAIL ICING

This is used to create the fine details on your cookies. When mixing up this icing, you'll know it's the right consistency when it forms a peak that slowly falls.

ROYAL ICING BASE RECIPE

If you wish to use your own homemade royal icing, make sure you use good-quality egg whites. It will keep well in the fridge for several days, provided the surface is tightly covered with clingfilm.

WHAT YOU'LL NEED

1 egg white

200 g (7 oz) icing sugar

WHAT TO DO

1. Put the egg white in a bowl and beat lightly to break it up. Add half the icing sugar and beat until smooth.

2. Gradually work in the remaining icing sugar until the icing has a soft, smooth consistency that just holds its shape.

3. Depending on what consistency icing you need, add more water (a few drops at a time) or more icing sugar.

PIPING YOUR ICING

Piping is a skill that is easily mastered with a little practice, and the results are so rewarding. You'll start to work much faster the more piping you do.

PIPING BAGS

It's possible to buy reusable piping bags that come with nozzles, but if you're decorating a biscuit with multiple colours and consistencies of icing, that means a lot of washing up between colours! For the designs in this book I've used disposable piping bags, which you can trim the end of to be the exact size of tip you need, or you can use a reusable nozzle.

PIPING WITHOUT A NOZZLE

Some designs require the merest amount to be snipped off the end of the bag to create a thin line – this is particularly important if you're piping an outline or fine detail. Only snip off a very small amount of the tip first; you can always snip off more if the line is too thin.

1. Half-fill the piping bag with icing and firmly twist the open end together to secure.

2. Once filled and the end is twisted to seal, snip off the tip.

PIPING WITH A NOZZLE

A piping nozzle is not absolutely necessary, but it does give a cleaner, more precise shape that ultimately looks more professional. A no. 2 round piping nozzle works best for these designs.

1. Cut off the end about 2 cm (¾ in) from the point of the bag, and insert the piping nozzle in the piping bag.

2. Half-fill the piping bag with icing and firmly twist the open end together to secure.

LINES, DOTS AND BEADING

Below are a few of the basic piping techniques which will help you recreate the designs in this book. Practise different effects by applying different amounts of pressure and holding the bag at different angles.

PIPED LINES
Squeeze the piping bag gently, keeping the piping bag raised slightly above the cookie and work at a speed that suits you.

STRAIGHT LINES
Hold the piping bag at about 45 degrees and keep a constant pressure as you squeeze out the icing.

DOTS
Hold the bag vertically and squeeze out tiny amounts of icing, releasing the pressure before you lift the bag away.

DECORATIVE BEADING
Hold the bag at about 45 degrees, squeeze out a dot of icing, release the pressure, move the bag fractionally backward and squeeze another dot. Repeat, as required.

EQUIPMENT

Other than basic baking equipment and a piping bag, below are a few items that will make your decorating a bit easier.

COCKTAIL STICK

Use a cocktail stick to add the food colouring to the icing as you only need a tiny amount. Cocktail sticks are also perfect for marbling icing (see the recipes on page 60 and 64).

SPRAY BOTTLE

Use a spray bottle to add water when thinning down the icing; this way you have a lot more control over the amount you put in.

EDIBLE PEN

You may find it beneficial to use an edible pen to outline some of the more detailed designs before piping.

SILICONE SPATULA

Mix the colours in by hand with a silicone spatula. Using an electric mixer will add too much air.

SMALL PAINTBRUSH

You'll need a small paintbrush for adding detailing to some of the designs. You can buy these at cake-craft and cooking shops, and online.

WIRE RACK

Place your decorated cookies on a wire rack to dry completely once they are decorated.

TIPS AND TRICKS

Below are a few tips and tricks to keep in mind while decorating your cookies, to help you achieve the best results.

- Before you begin any of the cookie designs in this book, make sure your freshly baked cookies are completely cooled.

- You may find it easier to place your cookie on a wire rack before you add any icing, as any stray drips will then fall onto the counter underneath without affecting the overall design too much. Or, if you prefer, you can place your cookies on a sheet of parchment paper – this will make the cleaning-up process super speedy.

- Use food colouring gels rather than liquids as they won't affect the icing consistency and the colours will be more vivid.

- Once you have flooded the cookie with icing, give it a little shake to help the icing settle out evenly. Pop any air bubbles with a cocktail stick.

- It's important to let certain stages dry properly before icing adjoining areas or adding details – patience is key!

- Dilute colouring gels with vodka for painting on details. Don't use water, as you need a high alcohol content so it evaporates and dries quickly. You can also use flavouring extracts in place of the vodka if you prefer, but keep in mind that the colour of the extract may affect the final result. Almond extract is a good option, as it tends to be lighter in colour – just make sure it includes alcohol in the ingredients.

HEART CUTTER

PRETZEL

Cookie? Pretzel? Cookie? Pretzel? Why waste time deciding when you can just have both?! This design is an homage to a snack served at events like Oktoberfest. It looks brilliant but is super easy to make – all you need is one colour and a sprinkle of sugar to create the most delicious-looking pretzel. For an even more authentic-tasting pretzel cookie, sprinkle over a small pinch of cinnamon at the end. Make sure you do this from a height so that the cinnamon is sprinkled over evenly and doesn't look clumpy.

WHAT YOU'LL NEED

Brown flood icing

White sugar crystals

WHAT TO DO

1. Using the brown flood icing, pipe the outer sections of the pretzel. While the icing is still wet, sprinkle with the sugar crystals and leave to dry.

2. Finish by piping the cross-over parts in the middle of the pretzel, again sprinkling with the sugar crystals while the icing is still wet. Waiting for the outer sections to dry before piping the middle will ensure your pretzel has definition and that the different parts don't blend into each other.

TIP FOR A CHOCOLATEY VERSION OF THE PRETZELS, MAKE YOUR COOKIES WITH CHOCOLATE DOUGH (SEE PAGE 7) AND SCATTER OVER CHOCOLATE VERMICELLI RATHER THAN THE SUGAR CRYSTALS.

VERY BERRY

This sumptuous summer berry is just perfect on a heart-shaped cookie, and is even better than the real thing. To make these cookies even sweeter, add a few drops of strawberry flavouring to the icing. Bear in mind that red can sometimes be a tricky colour to work with, so don't be afraid to add a little more food colouring to make your strawberries really pop.

WHAT YOU'LL NEED

Green piping icing

Red flood icing

Light yellow detail icing

WHAT TO DO

1. Using the green piping icing, pipe the leaves for your strawberry, allowing each leaf to dry before piping the adjoining one. This will ensure your leaves are nice and defined, and that they won't blend into each other.

2. Using the red flood icing, outline around the leaves and the edge of the cookie and fill it in. Leave to dry completely.

3. Pipe on your strawberry's seeds using the yellow detail icing. To create the seed shape, pipe a dot, then draw the piping bag down towards you as you finish piping to create a teardrop shape. This can be a little tricky at first, so practise on a piece of parchment paper beforehand.

ICE-CREAM CONE

You can almost taste strawberry ice cream just by looking at these adorable cookies. They're perfect by themselves, or stuck into a scoop of your favourite ice cream – they'd also make the most amazing ice-cream sandwiches. If you want to take things one step further, add a few drops of strawberry flavouring to the pink icing before piping it onto your cookie.

WHAT YOU'LL NEED

Light beige detail icing

Pink flood icing

Rainbow sugar strands

WHAT TO DO

1. Making sure to use a fine-tipped nozzle in your piping bag (or, if you aren't using a piping nozzle, cut only a very small hole in your piping bag), use the light beige detail icing to pipe the criss-cross lines of the waffle cone. Leave to dry completely.

2. Using the pink flood icing, pipe the outline of the pink ice cream and flood. You can go for a neat line where the ice cream meets the waffle cone, or you can add lots of drips to make your ice-cream cookies look all the more tempting.

3. While the icing is still wet, sprinkle over the rainbow sugar strands.

SLAM DUNK

Here's one for the sports-mad people in your life. I've gone for basketballs here, but you can just as easily do any sports ball you want. How about yellow with white lines for a tennis ball? Or white with black bits for a classic football design? Or perhaps baseballs with a white background and red stitching? Whatever you go for, these cookies are sure to knock all others out of the park.

WHAT YOU'LL NEED

Orange flood icing

Black detail icing

WHAT TO DO

1. Use the orange flood icing to pipe the outline of your basketball, then flood the centre and allow to dry completely.

2. Use the black detail icing to pipe on the lines.

TIP FOR AN EVEN MORE EXCITING VERSION OF YOUR BASKETBALL COOKIES, ALLOW THE BLACK LINES ON THE BASKETBALLS TO DRY COMPLETELY, THEN USE WHITE DETAIL ICING TO PIPE THIN CRISS-CROSS LINES OF BASKETBALL-HOOP NETTING OVER THE BOTTOM THIRD OF EACH BASKETBALL.

OVER THE RAINBOW

Rainbows are awesome in every way. They represent hope and happiness, and light up the sky on rainy days. They're also, of course, a symbol of Pride, which is usually celebrated yearly in June, but these cookies will keep the party going all year long. They look especially striking on a plain cookie, but you can always fill in the background – before you pipe your rainbow design – if you want.

WHAT YOU'LL NEED (SEE TIP)

Red piping icing

Orange piping icing

Yellow piping icing

Green piping icing

Blue piping icing

Purple piping icing

WHAT TO DO

1. Pipe a stripe of red icing, then leave to dry completely before piping the orange stripe.

2. Continue with the remaining colours, ensuring the previous colour is dry before piping the next.

TIP FOR THIS RECIPE, ADD A LITTLE MORE ICING SUGAR TO YOUR PIPING ICING SO THAT IT'S A BIT STIFFER. THIS WILL HELP THE ICING TO DRY FASTER IN BETWEEN PIPING THE STRIPES OF COLOUR SO THAT THEY DON'T RUN INTO EACH OTHER. THE PERFECT CONSISTENCY OF ICING FOR THIS COOKIE WILL TAKE ABOUT 25 SECONDS TO SETTLE INTO A FLAT LAYER.

BOOBS AND BUMS

These gorgeous, curvaceous cookies are sure to put a smile on anyone's face. Experiment with your own colours and patterns for bootylicious bikinis and lavish lingerie. Add a cheeky tattoo here, some pretty freckles there – whatever you can think of to give your cookies some personality. And don't forget – when it comes to making the bums, chop off the pointy end of the heart before sticking your cookies in the oven.

WHAT YOU'LL NEED

Mint green flood icing

Mint green detail icing

Light pink flood icing

Light pink detail icing

Light yellow flood icing

Light yellow detail icing

White detail icing

WHAT TO DO

1. For the boobs, use the flood icing in the colour of your choice to outline the bra cup, then fill it in and leave to dry completely.

2. Use detail icing in a matching colour (or have fun by switching up the colours) to pipe the strap and details on the bra.

3. For the bums, use flood icing in your chosen colour to outline the underwear, then fill it in and leave to dry completely.

4. Use detail icing in a matching or contrasting colour to pipe on the details – think lace and ribbon. Go wild and use your favourite pair as inspiration!

TWIT-TWOO

Now these cookies really are a hoot (sorry) – they're super quick and easy to make, and you can use whichever colours you have on hand and still get a perfect result. These cookies don't require lots of icing, so are great for people with slightly less of a sweet tooth.

WHAT YOU'LL NEED

White piping icing

Yellow piping icing

Black piping icing

Orange piping icing

Red detail icing

Yellow detail icing

Green detail icing

Blue detail icing

Brown detail icing

WHAT TO DO

1. Using the white piping icing, pipe the large circles for the owl's eyes. While the icing is still wet, use the yellow and black piping icing to create the pupils and allow to dry completely.

2. Then use the orange piping icing to pipe on your owl's beak.

3. Use the detail icing to pipe on the feathers around the eyes, alternating between red and yellow or green and blue.

4. Finally, finish off your owl by using the brown detail icing to pipe on its inquisitive eyebrows.

TIP THIS DESIGN LOOKS GREAT ON LIGHTER OR DARKER COLOURED COOKIES, BUT YOU COULD ALSO EXPERIMENT BY FLOODING THE BACKGROUND OF YOUR COOKIE IN WHICHEVER COLOUR YOU FANCY BEFORE PIPING ON YOUR OWL DESIGN.

FABULOUS FLAMINGO

If you're looking for a bold cookie design, look no further than these hot-pink, fabulous flamingos. If you're feeling extra fancy, you can finish your flamingo's feathers with a flourish of pink edible glitter. Or, completely change it up by using white icing for the feathers, black icing for the face and orange icing for the beak, for a graceful and elegant swan cookie design instead.

WHAT YOU'LL NEED

Bright pink flood icing

White piping icing

Light pink piping icing

Black piping icing

Bright pink detail icing

TIP FOR FLAVOURED FLAMINGOES, REPLACE THE VANILLA EXTRACT IN THE COOKIE RECIPE ON PAGE 6 WITH RASPBERRY OR STRAWBERRY FOOD FLAVOURING.

WHAT TO DO

1. Using the bright pink flood icing, pipe the outline of the flamingo, fill it in and leave to dry completely.

2. Using the white piping icing, pipe the white around your flamingo's eye and leave to dry.

3. Now use the light pink and black piping icing to pipe the beak, allowing each colour to crust over before doing the next.

4. Use the black piping icing to pipe your flamingo's eye.

5. Finish off your flamingo using the bright pink detail icing to pipe thin lines for its feathers.

LADYBIRD

Who can resist making a wish on these delightful little bugs? If you're anything like me, and all you wish for is cookies and more cookies, then you're in luck. This gorgeous design looks impressive, but is actually pretty easy to do. Plus, these little guys come in lots of different colours with different numbers of spots, so get creative and create your very own one-of-a-kind ladybird.

WHAT YOU'LL NEED

Black detail icing

Black flood icing

Red flood icing

White piping icing

WHAT TO DO

1. Using the black detail icing, pipe the outline of your ladybird.

2. Use the black flood icing to fill in the black section of the head and leave to dry.

3. Next, fill in your ladybird's wings with the red flood icing. While the icing is still wet, use the black flood icing to pipe on the dots.

4. Fill in the white details on the head with the white piping icing.

5. Finish off your ladybird by using the black detail icing to draw the raised outline down the centre of the wings.

YOU GIVE ME BUTTERFLIES

These beautiful, bright butterflies are a little more complicated to make, but so worth the stunning results. Once you have the basic outline down, the sky's the limit. Recreate your favourite butterfly from nature or invent your own design using your favourite colours.

WHAT YOU'LL NEED

Black flood icing

Yellow flood icing

Orange flood icing

White flood icing

Black detail icing

WHAT TO DO

1. Start by piping the black edge of your butterfly's main top wing using the black flood icing, then alternate between the yellow and orange flood icing to fill the rest of the wing.

2. While the icing is still wet, use a cocktail stick to drag the black icing through the yellow and orange. Then, while the icing is still wet, pipe on the white dots.

3. Use a cocktail stick to dot on the finer white details on the black part of the wing. For the larger dots at the top, start with white and add a dot of yellow in the centre.

4. Repeat this step for the bottom wing and the back top wing.

5. Once the wings have completely dried, use the black detail icing to pipe an outline around the wings, before finally piping the body and antenna.

GINGERBREAD
MAN CUTTER

ALIEN INVASION

We are not alone... Nothing incites fear quite like the classic bug-eyed green alien – the stuff of childhood (...and fully grown adult) nightmares. For this cookie design, it doesn't matter if your piping skills aren't that great, as the weirder these guys look, the better. Which also means they're super quick and easy for days when you don't have as much patience. And you don't have to go for green either – mix it up by playing with purples, greys and blues for truly out-of-this-world cookies.

WHAT YOU'LL NEED

Green piping icing

Black detail icing

WHAT TO DO

1. Use the green piping icing to pipe the outline of the alien, then fill it in and leave to dry completely. Experiment by giving your alien wiggly limbs – they don't need to look perfect.

2. Finish off your alien by piping on the eyes with the black detail icing.

TIP BAKE YOUR WAY INTO ANY SCI-FI LOVER'S HEART WITH A PLATE OF THESE ALIENS TOGETHER WITH THE GALAXIES ON PAGE 64 AND THE ASTRONAUTS ON PAGE 41.

ASTRONAUT

Go boldly where no one has ever gone before with this awesome space-faring astronaut cookie. No matter what the occasion is, these guys are ready for launch. Try pairing them with the alien cookie design on page 39 or the galaxy design on page 64 for the ultimate space-themed cookie box. One small step for man, perhaps, but a giant leap in your cookie-decorating game.

WHAT YOU'LL NEED

White flood icing

Grey flood icing

Grey detail icing

White detail icing

Red detail icing

Green detail icing

WHAT TO DO

1. Using the white flood icing, pipe the outline of the white areas of the astronaut's space suit, then fill them in and allow to dry completely. Then do the same with the grey areas of the space suit.

2. Use the grey detail icing to outline the boots, belt, helmet and gloves. Then use the white detail icing to pipe on the sleeves and buttons.

3. Pipe two little rectangles in red and green detail icing for your astronaut's badge.

4. For a final touch, use the white detail icing to pipe the highlight on your astronaut's visor.

ZOMBIE ATTACK

This spooky take on a gingerbread man is especially useful for when you've accidentally broken some of the cookies (or if you just couldn't resist taking a bite... Hey, it happens to the best of us). Just add a bit of red icing to the edge and ta-da! No one will ever know. This design is great for those who prefer their cookies with a bit less icing – it's also super quick and easy to do, but still looks great.

WHAT YOU'LL NEED

Red detail icing

White detail icing

Black detail icing

WHAT TO DO

1. Begin by snapping off the leg, head or arm of your gingerbread man (be as brutal as you like!) and pipe a thin line of red detail icing along the broken edge.

2. For the stitches, use a cocktail stick to carve a line across the gingerbread man, being careful not to go too deep or you'll snap it.

3. Then use the white detail icing to pipe small lines or crosses across the carved line to create stitches.

4. Finish your zombie off by piping on its eyes. Pipe one larger than the other for that unsettling zombie stare.

MUMMY MAYHEM

Everyone's favourite movie monster just got a whole load cuter – and more delicious. This design uses fondant icing, so if you go slightly wrong, just roll it back up and start again. These guys are pretty friendly looking, but if that doesn't quite cut it for you, and you want to make them a little more terrifying, use red or yellow icing for the eyes and add the odd blood-stained bandage here and there.

WHAT YOU'LL NEED

White flood icing

White fondant icing

White detail icing

Black detail icing

WHAT TO DO

1. Using the white flood icing, outline the cookie, then fill it in (leaving a gap for the eyes) and leave to dry completely.

2. While you are waiting for your cookie to dry, roll the fondant out to around 3–4 mm (⅛ in) thick and cut it into strips.

3. Brush a little water onto the strips of fondant to help them stick, then lay them across the iced cookie to create the bandages.

4. Finally, pipe on eyes using the white detail icing, before adding a small dot of black detail icing for each pupil.

MONSTERA

What's better than a beautiful new houseplant? An edible version, of course – and these cookies are just as gorgeous as the real thing. You can mix things up by changing the colour and pattern on the flowerpot – try edible glitter or coloured sugars. If you're feeling ambitious, you can also try a range of different plants, such as a fern or a cactus.

WHAT YOU'LL NEED

Green detail icing

Green piping icing

White piping icing

Rainbow sprinkles

WHAT TO DO

1. Using the green detail icing, outline the leaves. Then use the green piping icing to fill them in, and also for the branches, making sure all the leaves are connected to the main stem. Leave these to dry completely.

2. Then, using the green detail icing, pipe a thin, raised outline around the leaves to give them more definition.

3. Next, use white piping icing to outline and fill the pot.

4. Finally, while the icing is still wet, cover it with rainbow sprinkles to give your flower pot a pretty and unique design.

OCTOPUS

This stunning, colourful octopus cookie is an absolute favourite of mine. Embrace these guys' natural colour-changing abilities and try out every colour combination you can think of – get creative and go mad! For the ultimate under-the-sea themed cookie box, match these cookies up with the starfish on page 74 and the sharks on page 53.

WHAT YOU'LL NEED

Orange flood icing

White piping icing

Black detail icing

Light orange flood icing

Dark purple detail icing

Light purple flood icing

TIP USE THE PHOTO AS GUIDANCE TO DECORATE YOUR OCTOPUS COOKIES IN OTHER COLOURWAYS.

WHAT TO DO

1. Use the orange flood icing to pipe the outline of the octopus, then fill it in and allow to dry completely.

2. Use the white piping icing to draw in the eyes. While the icing is still wet, pipe a ring in black detail icing for each pupil.

3. Use the light orange flood icing to fill in the back tentacles and leave to dry completely.

4. Use the dark purple detail icing to add the tentacle suckers and details on the head. Don't worry about making these perfect – they'll look better if they're all slightly different sizes!

5. While the icing is still wet, pipe a dot of light purple flood icing in the centre of each sucker.

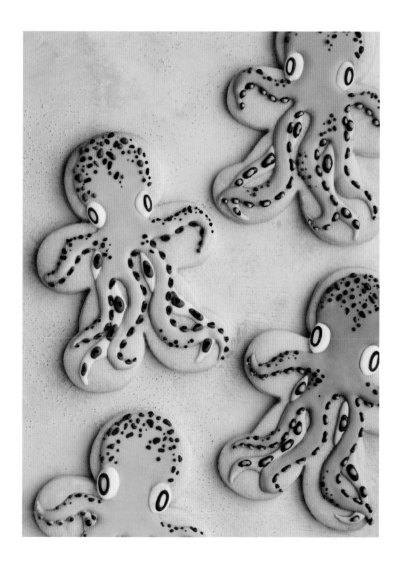

PANDA-MONIUM

Now these cookies are sure to be an absolute crowd-pleaser. These adorably plump, bamboo-eating, black-and-white bears make for the cutest cookie. Not only is this design pretty quick and easy to do, it's also super versatile. Experiment with different colours to create a brown bear, a polar bear or even a pink teddy bear with multi-coloured polka dots. Just be warned – you may end up with something too cute to eat.

WHAT YOU'LL NEED

White flood icing

Black flood icing

Black detail icing

WHAT TO DO

1. Use the white flood icing to outline and fill the white areas on the face and body of your panda, and allow to dry completely.

2. Then use the black flood icing to fill in the ears, arms, feet and eye patches. While the icing for the eye patches is still wet, pipe on a small dot of white for each eye and follow with a smaller dot of black detail icing for the pupil.

3. Finish off your panda by piping on a cute nose using black detail icing.

JAWS

Da dum...da dum... Turn your gingerbread cookie on its side and recreate these fearsome great white sharks with their beady little eyes and iconic dorsal fins. To make your sharks extra terrifying, dot some blood-red icing on to the tips of their razor-sharp teeth. These guys would go great with the octopus design on page 48 and the starfish on page 74.

WHAT YOU'LL NEED

Light grey flood icing

White flood icing

Light grey detail icing

White detail icing

Red detail icing

Black detail icing

WHAT TO DO

1. Using the light grey flood icing, pipe the outline of your shark, then fill in the main grey area of the body, and leave to dry completely. Once the icing is dry, use the white flood icing to fill in the white areas in the same way, and leave to dry completely.

2. Next, use the light grey detail icing to outline the fin and gills.

3. Use white detail icing to pipe on the razor-sharp teeth and, once completely dry, add a thin line of blood across the teeth using the red detail icing.

4. Finally, use the black detail icing for your shark's beady eye.

FIESTA LLAMA

Do these llovely llittle llamas really need an introduction?
Just look at those oversized sunglasses and multi-coloured
pom-poms – who could be unhappy looking at that utterly
adorable face?

WHAT YOU'LL NEED (SEE TIP)

White flood icing

Light pink piping icing

Light pink flood icing

Black flood icing

White detail icing

Black detail icing

Green detail icing

Blue detail icing

Yellow detail icing

Red detail icing

TIP MAKE THE LIGHT PINK
PIPING ICING A BIT STIFFER FOR
THIS COOKIE. THIS WILL HELP
THE BOBBLES OF THE HAIR DRY
FASTER IN BETWEEN PIPING, AND
IT WILL BE MORE DEFINED. THE
PERFECT CONSISTENCY ICING
WILL TAKE ABOUT 25 SECONDS
TO SETTLE INTO A FLAT LAYER.

WHAT TO DO

1. Using the white flood icing, outline and fill the white areas on your llama's ears and nose, and allow to crust over.

2. Next, create the hair by piping dots of varying sizes with the light pink piping icing. Allow the icing to crust over before piping dots right next to each other to avoid them blending together.

3. Outline and fill the rest of the pink areas of the ears and face with the light pink flood icing.

4. Using the black flood icing, outline and fill the black areas of the sunglasses. While the icing is still wet, use the white detail icing to pipe a thin line for the reflection.

5. Use the black detail icing for your llama's nose, mouth and pom-pom string around the ear.

6. Once the black icing has fully dried, outline the glasses with the green detail icing and pipe dots in blue, yellow, red and green for the pom-poms.

RUDOLPH

If these reindeer cookies don't get you in the mood for Christmas, I don't know what will. I've chosen to decorate their antlers with a cute string of fairy lights, but you could do mistletoe or baubles if you like – just don't forget Rudolph's shining red nose. For the ultimate Christmas cookie gift box, you can pair these guys with the Santa cookies on page 72 or the mistletoe cookies on page 71.

WHAT YOU'LL NEED

Brown flood icing

Light pink piping icing

Light brown flood icing

Beige piping icing

Black detail icing

Red detail icing

Yellow detail icing

Orange detail icing

Blue detail icing

Green detail icing

WHAT TO DO

1. Using the brown flood icing, outline the main part of your reindeer's head, then fill it in and allow to crust over.

2. Then use the light pink piping icing to fill in the ears.

3. Now fill in the rest of the face with the light brown flood icing.

4. Using the beige piping icing, pipe the outline of the antlers, then fill them in and leave to dry completely.

5. Now for the festive fairy lights to adorn your reindeer's antlers: pipe the wire for the lights using the black detail icing, then use the detail icing in the remaining colours to pipe on the lightbulbs.

6. Finish your reindeer's face by piping on its eyes, eyebrows and nose.

STAR
CUTTER

CRYSTAL

Crystals are a source of healing therapeutic energy – and now you can eat them, too. These cookies are perfect paired up with the galaxy cookies on page 64 for a star-studded gift box.

WHAT YOU'LL NEED

Light grey flood icing

White flood icing

White piping icing

Clear boiled sweets, smashed into uneven shards

White sugar sprinkles

Edible gold paint

Purple gel food colouring

Pink gel food colouring

Blue gel food colouring

Few drops vodka or flavouring extract

WHAT TO DO

1. Place the grey icing in a bowl large enough to dip the cookies in. Blob in spoonfuls of the white flood icing and gently swirl the two icings together with a cocktail stick to create a marbled effect. Be careful not to overmix the icing.

2. Dip each of the cookies into the marbled icing, being careful to keep them flat on the surface of the icing. Leave to dry.

3. Use the white piping icing to mark out where you want your crystal to be. While the icing is still wet, press on the crushed-up boiled sweets and leave to dry.

4. Using the white piping icing, pipe a line either side of the crystal. While the icing is still wet, sprinkle over the lines with the white sugar sprinkles. Leave to dry, then use the gold paint to give your crystal pretty lustred edges.

5. Place a couple drops of food colouring in a dish, and dilute with the vodka or flavouring extract. Use a paintbrush to dot the colour over the shards, concentrating the colour in the centre.

UNICORN

If you're anything like me and the sight of a flower crown
and a golden-lustered horn fills you with complete joy, you
simply must have a go at these gorgeous unicorn cookies.
Or unicookies, if you will. Don't worry if you can't find
any edible gold lustre dust – your cookies will look just
as magical without.

WHAT YOU'LL NEED

White flood icing

Yellow flood icing

Beige detail icing

Gold lustre dust

Light pink detail icing

Light purple detail icing

Light yellow detail icing

Light green detail icing

Black detail icing

WHAT TO DO

1. Using the white flood icing, pipe the
   outline and flood the cookie. Carefully
   transfer it to a wire rack and leave to dry
   completely.

2. Use the yellow flood icing to fill the horn
   area and allow to dry. Then use the beige
   detail icing to pipe the shape and details
   onto the horn. Once dry, dust over some
   of the gold lustre dust to make your
   unicorn's horn sparkle.

3. Adorn your unicorn's horn with a pretty
   flower crown, using the light pink and
   light purple detail icing to pipe the petals
   and the light yellow detail icing for the
   centres. Then use the light green detail
   icing to add a few leaves.

4. Use the black detail icing to pipe on your
   unicorn's eyes.

GLORIOUS GALAXY

These cookies are utterly beautiful and look almost too good to eat. I know they look complicated, but don't be intimidated – this design is actually surprisingly easy to do. It's just a case of marbling different coloured icings through each other. Easy-peasy. You can experiment with all sorts of different colours too, like greens and blues. The white stars are the perfect finish, but for some extra sparkle you could always add a dusting of edible glitter.

WHAT YOU'LL NEED

White flood icing

Pink food colouring gel

Blue food colouring gel

Purple food colouring gel

Black food colouring gel

White edible paint

WHAT TO DO

1. Place the white flood icing in a bowl that is wide enough to dip the cookies in. Add drops of each of the food colouring gels to the icing, and use a cocktail stick to marble the colours through the icing. Be careful not to overmix the icing to ensure you don't lose the marbled effect.

2. Dip each cookie into the icing, being careful to keep them flat on the surface. As you pull the cookie away from the icing, the marbled food colouring will create the beautiful swirling galaxy effect. Carefully place the cookies on a wire rack to set completely.

3. Using a dry paintbrush, dip it in a little white edible paint and draw your fingertip through the bristles to splatter the paint and create stars.

TRIPPY TIE-DYE

This far-out tie-dye design is super easy to recreate, and the results are pretty darn groovy. For truly psychedelic cookies, experiment with different colour combinations that stand out from each other – like purple and yellow or orange and blue – or go for a full-on rainbow effect. Or, for something a little more mellow, try using the same colour but in different hues. Whatever you go for, the results are sure to be trippy.

WHAT YOU'LL NEED

Pink flood icing

Yellow flood icing

White flood icing

WHAT TO DO

1. Using the pink or yellow flood icing, pipe around the outer edge of the cookie.

2. Continue piping the outline of the star, alternating between pink, yellow and white flood icing, getting closer and closer to the centre of the cookie until you have filled the whole thing.

3. Use a cocktail stick to drag lines out from the centre of the still-wet icing to create the tie-die effect. Experiment by dragging out a different number of lines for each cookie – the more lines you drag out, the more detailed the design will look.

SPRING DAFFODIL

Nothing says spring is here quite like the sight of yellow daffodils peaking up through the grass, and these delightful cookies are guaranteed to put a spring in anyone's step. Celebrate the end of rubbish weather and dark days with these little rays of sunshine. You can match them with the ladybird cookies on page 33 and the butterflies on page 34 for a gorgeous spring-themed cookie box.

WHAT YOU'LL NEED

Orange flood icing

Yellow flood icing

Orange detail icing

Yellow gel food colouring

Few drops vodka or flavouring extract

WHAT TO DO

1. Using the orange flood icing, pipe the centre trumpet of your daffodil, then leave to crust over.

2. Use the yellow flood icing to pipe the petals, allowing them to crust over in between piping each one. This will ensure your petals are beautifully defined and don't blend into each other.

3. Using the orange detail icing, pipe the ruffle on the trumpet and stamens and leave to dry completely.

4. Place a few drops of yellow gel food colouring in a small dish and water down with a few drops of vodka or flavouring extract. Use a small paintbrush to brush streaks of yellow onto the petals to create definition.

UNDER THE MISTLETOE

Rumour has it that if you hold these cookies over your head, you might get a little sugar this Christmas... and I'm not talking about the cookies. Try pairing these beauties with the Santa cookie on page 72 and the Rudolph cookie on page 56 for the perfect Christmas-themed cookie box.

WHAT YOU'LL NEED

Green piping icing

Green detail icing

White detail icing

Red detail icing

WHAT TO DO

1. Using the green piping icing, pipe the leaves in a curved teardrop shape characteristic of mistletoe leaves. Make sure to leave each leaf to crust over before piping any others that are touching. This will ensure that your leaves are clearly defined and don't blend into each other. Make sure you fill each corner of your star cookie to create the effect of a beautiful big bunch of mistletoe.

2. Use the green detail icing to pipe the branches, making sure all the mistletoe leaves are connected to one main branch at the top of the cookie.

3. Using the white detail icing, pipe on the berries. Alternate the number of berries you pipe on each leaf for a more natural effect.

4. Use the red detail icing to finish off your cookie with a gorgeously festive red bow.

SANTA'S COMING TO TOWN

Whether you've been naughty or nice, it's time for a little holiday cheer, and these Santa cookies are just the thing. Paired with the Rudolph cookies on page 56 and the mistletoe cookies on page 71, they make the perfect Christmas gift box. Or, you could even leave them out by the fireplace on Christmas Eve for the big man himself.

WHAT YOU'LL NEED

Red flood icing

White piping icing

Light pink piping icing

White detail icing

Black detail icing

Yellow detail icing

WHAT TO DO

1. Using the red flood icing, pipe your Santa's suit and hat. Carefully place the cookie on a wire rack and leave the icing to crust over.

2. Use the white piping icing to pipe Santa's big bushy beard and leave to dry completely.

3. Fill in his face using the light pink piping icing and allow to crust over before piping on his nose.

4. Use the white detail icing to pipe your Santa's moustache and eyebrows, before piping his cuffs and the fluffy edge and pom-pom on his hat.

5. Pipe your Santa's gloves, shoes, belt and eyes with the black detail icing, and his golden, shining belt buckle with the yellow detail icing.

SENSATIONAL STARFISH

Journey under the sea with these stunning starfish cookies. This design may look intricate, but it's pretty much just a case of piping different-sized dots onto your cookie. Use colours that really stand out against each other, like the hot pink and neon blue pictured opposite. These cookies will go great with the octopus design on page 48 and the shark on page 53.

WHAT YOU'LL NEED

Bright pink flood icing

Turquoise detail icing

WHAT TO DO

1. Using the bright pink flood icing, outline and fill in your starfish. Carefully place the starfish on a wire rack and leave the icing to dry completely.

2. Use the turquoise detail icing to pipe each starfish's details. Experiment with alternating between larger and smaller dots to give your starfish a beautifully intricate look.

TIP FOR A COMPLETE SEASIDE LOOK, DISPLAY YOUR STARFISH ON EDIBLE 'SAND'. YOU CAN USE GROUND ALMONDS OR BROWN SUGAR BUT, FOR THE MOST EFFECTIVE-LOOKING 'SAND', BLITZ DIGESTIVE BISCUITS IN A FOOD PROCESSOR OR PLACE IN A SEALABLE PLASTIC FOOD BAG AND BASH WITH A ROLLING PIN UNTIL THE BISCUITS ARE REDUCED TO A SANDY RUBBLE.

COOL CATS

Didn't think the purr-fect cookie existed? Well think again. These kitties, with their movie-star sunglasses and perfect pouts, are the coolest cats on the block. Play around with colours and patterns to recreate your favourite feline friend.

WHAT YOU'LL NEED

Light pink flood icing

Orange flood icing

White flood icing

Light grey flood icing

Black detail icing

Black flood icing

Green detail icing

Red detail icing

Blue detail icing

Orange gel food colouring
(for a ginger cat)

Black gel food colouring
(for a grey cat)

Few drops vodka or flavouring
extract

WHAT TO DO

1. Using the light pink flood icing, pipe the pink of the ears and leave to crust over.

2. Now, pipe the orange, white and light grey parts of your cat's face using flood icing in each of the colours. Make sure to leave each section to crust over before piping the adjoining section so the colours don't blend into each other.

3. Once completely dry, use the black detail icing to give your cat a nose and some whiskers.

4. Fill the black parts of the glasses in using the black flood icing and leave to dry.

5. Pipe the outline of the glasses using detail icing in green, red or blue.

6. Place a few drops of gel food colouring in a dish and dilute with the vodka or flavouring extract. Test the colour on a piece of kitchen paper first, and if the colour is too dark, dilute it further. Use a paintbrush to brush on faint stripes to create a tabby effect.

PARTY PUPS

These little pups – with their party hats, bow ties and neckerchiefs – are sure to melt your heart. The points of the star cookie leave plenty of room for even the perkiest of puppy ears, so experiement with all kinds of dogs or recreate your very own. Just don't forget to add fun accessories for some bow-wow bling.

FRENCH BULL DOG

WHAT YOU'LL NEED

Light pink piping icing

White piping icing

Light grey piping icing

Black detail icing

White detail icing

Green detail icing

WHAT TO DO

1. Using light pink piping icing, pipe the pink part of the ears. Then, using the white piping icing, pipe the bottom triangle of the mouth and leave to dry.

2. Outline the grey part of face using the light grey piping icing, fill in and leave to dry.

3. Pipe the remaining white part of the face using the white piping icing, leaving a thin line between each section to create the mouth.

4. Use the white piping icing to fill in the eyes, and while it's wet, use the black detail icing for the pupils and the white detail icing to highlight them – pipe the white onto a cocktail stick first, and use this to dot onto the pupils.

5. Use the black detail icing for the nose. Then, pipe the centre dot of the bow tie using the green detail icing and allow to dry before piping the sides.

SHIBA INU

WHAT YOU'LL NEED

Orange piping icing

White piping icing

Black detail icing

Red piping icing

White detail icing

WHAT TO DO

1. Using the orange piping icing, outline and fill the orange part of the face and leave to dry. Then, using the white piping icing, fill in the white parts of the face and ears.

2. Use the black icing for the eyes and nose, then pipe the scarf using the red icing. While it's still wet, pipe some cute polka dots using the white detail icing. Finish with a smile, using the black icing.

PUG

WHAT YOU'LL NEED

Dark brown piping icing

Light brown piping icing

Black detail icing

White detail icing

Light pink piping icing

Light brown detail icing

WHAT TO DO

1. Using the dark brown icing, pipe the ears and bottom of the mouth and leave to dry. Then pipe the left side of the mouth, leaving to dry before piping the right.

2. Using the light brown piping icing, outline the eyes (leaving them blank), fill in the rest of the face and leave to dry.

3. Still using the light brown piping icing, fill in the eyes. While it's still wet, use the black icing to pipe the pupils and the white detail icing to highlight them – pipe the white onto a cocktail stick first, and use this to dot onto the pupils.

4. Using the light pink piping icing, outline and fill the hat. While it's still wet, use the white detail icing to pipe the spots. Then, use the black detail icing for the nose and the light brown detail icing to pipe the wrinkles on its forehead.